LIONS

By Sophie Lockwood

Content Adviser: Barbara E. Brown, Scientific Associate, Mammal Division, Field Museum of Chicago

THE CHILD'S WORLD®, MANKATO, MINNESOTA

Lions

Published in the United States of America by The Child's World®
1980 Lookout Drive • Mankato, MN 56003-1705
800-599-READ • www.childsworld.com

Acknowledgements:

The Child's World®: Mary Berendes, Publishing Director

The Creative Spark: Mary Francis, Project Director; Wendy Mead, Editor; Deborah Goodsite, Photo Researcher

The Design Lab: Kathleen Petelinsek, Designer and Production Artist

Photos:

Cover: Kevdog818/iStockphoto.com; frontispiece and page 4: Kristian Sekulic/iStockphoto.com; half title: Nico Smit/iStockphoto.com.

Interior: Alamy: 30 (SCPhotos); Animals Animals/Earth Scenes: 5 top left and 9 (Johnny Johnson), 5 bottom right and 29 (David Tipling/OSF); The Art Archive: 5 bottom left and 33 (Archaeological Museum Djemila Algeria/Dagli Orti); Getty Images: 5 top right and 13 (Manoj Shah/Stone), 16–17 (Theo Allofs/Photonica), 18 (Beverly Joubert/National Geographic), 27 (S. Purdy Matthews/Stone); Minden Pictures: 21 (Winfried Wisniewski/FLPA), 22 (Suzi Eszterhas); Photolibrary Group: 10; SuperStock: 15 (age fotostock), 5 center left and 24 (Christophe Courteau/TMC); Photo Researchers, Inc.: 36–37 (Christophe Ratier).

Library of Congress Cataloging-in-Publication Data

Lockwood, Sophie.
  Lions / by Sophie Lockwood.
    p. cm. — (The world of mammals)
  ISBN 978-1-59296-933-3 (library bound : alk. paper)
  1. Lions—Juvenile literature. I. Title. II. Series.
  QL737.C23L63 2008
  599.757—dc22   2007013567

TABLE OF CONTENTS

Chapter One

Along the Mara River

The September sun beats down on the **savanna** along the Mara River. In the shade of a grove of acacia trees, lions enjoy a deep, peaceful sleep. They are waiting, these lions. This is the time when more than two million wildebeest move from the Serengeti Plain into the Masai Mara region—the lion's neighborhood. Tonight, the lions will hunt and fill their bellies. For now, it is enough to just sleep.

The land along the Mara is ideal for lions. High cliffs overlook swaths of dense green. Black-and-white-striped zebras graze on the fresh grass. Elephants trample a wide path to the river for a drink and a spray of cooling water. Nearby, African buffalo wallow in the muddy shallows. Antelope browse the green shoots that popped up after the rains. Odd-looking, bearded wildebeest cluster together, exhausted from crossing the river and dodging dangerous Nile crocodiles. This is a lion's all-you-can-eat buffet.

There is plenty of **prey** to be hunted, and lions are not the only hunters on the

Would You Believe?
Lions can sleep up to 20 to 21 hours a day. The choice of a good sleeping spot is important, and many lions nap in the shade of trees or overhanging rocks, or even up in trees.

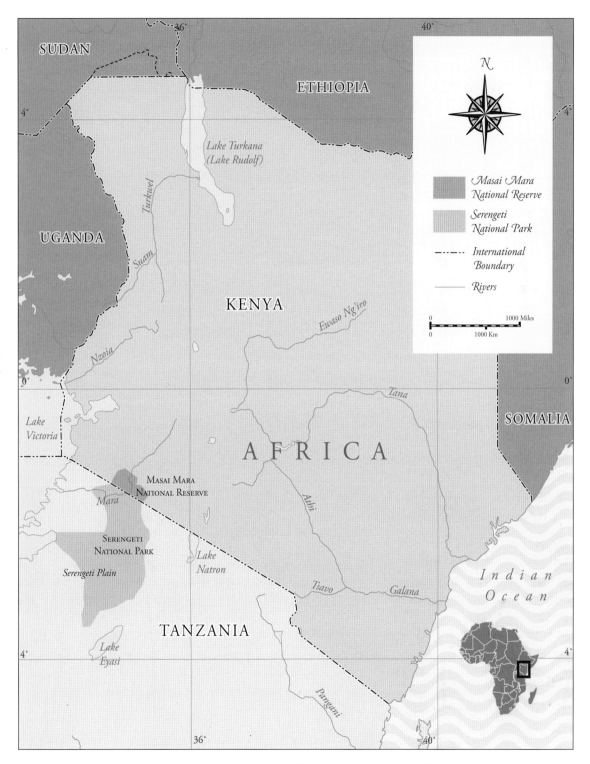

People travel from around the world to see the lions of Masai Mara.

Mara **escarpment.** Leopards stalk impalas in the tall grasses. Racing at speeds up to 95 kilometers per hour (60 miles per hour), cheetahs chase down swift, darting gazelles. A family of jackals searches through the croton bushes for warthog piglets—a favorite snack. These hunters do not directly affect lions because the larger cats prefer to hunt larger prey. A gazelle is a full meal plus leftovers for a cheetah, but barely a nibble for a **pride** of lions.

Then there is the lion's greatest enemy—spotted hyenas. Hyenas, African wild dogs, and lions compete for prey. These three **predator** species hunt in groups and choose similar prey. While lions enjoy their status as top predators, hyenas simply see lions as convenient food suppliers. After the lions catch a zebra, hyenas sometimes steal it away. It is hard to imagine the king of beasts being chased away from dinner, but packs of hyenas are fearless and vicious.

THE HUNT

Here in Masai Mara, male lions have only a few jobs to do, and protecting the pride's territory is one of them. As the sun sets, the pride's males roar. The sound echoes across the plains. Both male and female lions roar, but it is the

male's deep-voiced roar that carries for miles. The message is clear: *If you hear this, you are in my space. Get out!* Males do not want other lions hunting in their territory—a job that usually belongs to the pride's females, called lionesses.

Darkness falls abruptly on the African savanna. For the lionesses, it is time to go

A male lion's roar sends a clear signal—go away!

Would You Believe?
Lions that live along the Savuti River often prey on young elephants. Along the Linyanti River, prides hunt hippopotamuses.

grocery shopping. Lionesses are smaller, faster, and not as easily seen as the bulkier, full-maned males. This lion pride consists of three males, seven females, and a dozen cubs. That adds up to twenty-two mouths to feed.

A pride of lions enjoy a meal of zebra.

Lions have developed an excellent hunting strategy. Tonight, five of the pride's lionesses hunt together. This will be a direct assault using an age-old strategy. Four lionesses go to the far side of the herd of wildebeests and wait.

One lioness moves close to the herd and roars. The wildebeests stampede in panic—heading straight toward the waiting lionesses. The frightened wildebeests run for their lives. The lionesses pick out young, old, slow, or sickly beasts. A wildebeest separates from the herd. The lionesses are ready.

Lions can run at speeds up to 64 kilometers per hour (40 miles per hour) in short bursts. The lionesses expend all their energy getting close, then leap onto their prey. They bite the prey's neck to bring it down. Only one lioness is successful in tonight's hunt. Still, she brings down an adult with a wounded leg that weighs about 180 kilograms (nearly 400 pounds).

The male lions arrive as soon as the hunt is over, along with the other females and older cubs. The hungry cats growl, snarl, and jockey for space at the carcass. The males eat first, followed by the females. Cubs eat last and sometimes get no food at all. Tonight, everyone eats.

Did You Know?
Adult male lions can weigh twice what adult females weigh. The average male lion weighs 150 to 250 kilograms (330 to 550 pounds), while females usually weigh 80 to 150 kilograms (200 to 300 pounds). The males' extra weight makes them slower than lionesses—a disadvantage when hunting animals on the run.

Chapter Two

A Lion's Pride

Lions are the only cats that live in social groups. A pride can be any size from two to thirty or more. Numbers generally depend on the amount of food available in the pride's territory. While prides have many females and cubs, males usually number two or four, but rarely five or more.

The core of the pride is its female population. The lionesses are usually all related—mother, daughters, sisters, and granddaughters. During their twelve-year **life span** in the wild, most lionesses remain with their birth prides.

Males take the "lion's share" of every catch they find, but they face great danger during their lives. Protecting the pride and its territory requires fighting off invaders. Repeated battles over territory and the pride leave males scarred and weakened. Males rarely live past ten years old.

A male cub lives with the pride until he reaches two or three years old. Then, the older males force the young one to leave. If the male is lucky, he has brothers or male cousins of the same age who

Would You Believe?
The lion is called the "king of the jungle," but the jungle is one place lions do *not* live. It is too hard to find and hunt prey in a dense jungle.

leave at the same time. The young males form a partnership, called a **coalition,** and live a **nomadic** life for two or three years. At five years old, males are fully mature and ready to head up a pride.

Founding a new pride is not easy. The male coalition must find females. The newly formed pride needs a hunting territory—and the best spots are already taken.

A mother looks after her cub for the first few years of its life.

A pride's home range can be from 20 to 400 square kilometers (7.7 to 154 square miles), depending on the amount of prey available. The ideal home range has a year-round mix of prey—antelope, oryx, African buffalo, warthog, zebra, giraffe, and wildebeest.

TAKING OVER A PRIDE

It is somewhat easier to take over an existing pride than to set up a new one. A coalition roams through the region looking for a pride with older male lions. Challenging five- or six-year-old males for rights to a pride usually ends in defeat. If a pride's males are in the eight- to nine-year-old range, however, the young males have a good chance of beating the older, weaker defenders.

The battle for control is vicious. Claws and teeth cause painful wounds, and losing the fight can be deadly. Often male lions get so badly injured that they die from their wounds. Some face starvation because they are too weak to hunt. All too often, they become the prey of a band of cackling hyenas.

The young males immediately establish themselves as leaders in their newly gained pride. They must ensure that their **genes** are carried on in the pride's

young. To do so, they kill all nursing cubs. Death at the hands of adult males accounts for one in three cub deaths before age two in the Masai Mara region.

This seems shocking, but it is the way of nature. Males have a short time to rule the pride. In two or three years, another coalition will challenge and drive out the reigning kings. If a lioness already has a litter of nursing cubs, she

A young male lion will fight an older male for control of a pride.

Male and female African lions have different responsibilities within the pride.

will not breed again for nearly two years. However, if she loses her cubs, she will come into **estrus** within a couple of weeks. Estrus is a period of time during which a female is sexually ready to mate with a male. Females in estrus have a scent that males recognize. The new pride leader can then mate with the female and sire young.

Mating requires endurance. A lion and lioness will mate three to four times an hour, twenty-four hours a day, for two to three days. The lion's roars fill the air, day and night. It is necessary to mate this frequently to guarantee that a female gets pregnant during the time she is in estrus. Females go into estrus several times a year, but only one fertile period in five results in pregnancy.

SOCIAL MANNERS

Although their attitude toward outsiders is definitely unfriendly, pride lions do not squabble among themselves. There are good reasons to be easygoing within the pride. An adult lion can cause serious harm in a fight. Males must conserve their energy for defending the pride against intruders. Females use their efforts to raise young and to hunt. Fighting with each other would weaken the pride and decrease its chance for survival.

Would You Believe?
When a male lion roars, the sound can be heard for 8 kilometers (5 miles).

Lions can "talk" with each other using sounds and gestures.

Lions spend their days resting, sleeping, flicking away flies, and sleeping a bit more. On occasion, one lion will groom another with its sandpaper-rough tongue. Lions cannot afford to be too active—activity uses up energy. Unlike zebras or giraffes, lions do not eat every day. Without a daily food supply, lions wisely conserve their energy.

As social animals, lions must communicate well with each other. They do so with gestures and sounds. Lions give visual cues, such as taking a specific stance or making a facial gesture, toward each other. When an unwelcome visitor arrives, a male lion takes on an aggressive or defensive posture. With teeth bared and mane standing on end, the male sends a clear warning. Males also mark their territories by spraying **urine** on plants or scuff-marking trees.

Male lions develop the ability to roar at about one year old (females a bit later), and roaring says plenty. It advertises territory ownership, warns strange lions to stay away, and communicates among pride members. Often, a chorus of roars cuts through the twilight. The pride members are telling each other where they are and what they are doing.

Chapter Three

A Close Bond

A four-year-old lioness prowls the outskirts of the pride's territory. Her belly sways from side to side, bulky with a litter of cubs. Her fourteen-week pregnancy will soon be over, but for now, she is uncomfortable.

The birth is near. **Instinctively,** the new mother looks for a quiet spot among the croton bushes, where she can deliver her young. Collapsing to the ground, she settles on her side and waits.

Her first cub is born during the night. She gently lifts it with her teeth by the scruff of the neck. She licks the cub to clean it and nudges it toward a nipple. The first cub is already nursing when his brother is born. After two male cubs are born, a female arrives an hour later.

The cubs weigh between 1 and 2 kilograms (2.2 and 4.4 pounds). With eyes yet to open, the speckled gray-tan cubs grope blindly to latch onto the mother's nipples and drink her rich milk. Mother will keep the cubs away from the pride until they are six to

Would You Believe?
In the Samburu National Reserve in Kenya, a lioness that locals named Kamuniak has adopted five oryx calves and one impala over several years. Oryx are normally lion prey, but Kamuniak, which means "Blessed One," chose to mother these infants.

eight weeks old. During the time alone, a strong bond forms between mother and children.

Dangers to small cubs are many, and the mother lion watches for possible problems. Mongooses, pythons, eagles, leopards, jackals, wild dogs, and the dreaded hyenas will gladly feast on a lion cub. On occasion, cubs might come into contact with nervous African buffalo. Bulls are known to gore lions and cubs with their horns. A lioness, finding the body of her dead cub, may eat it. This is natural for a **carnivore.** Nature does not waste food.

A lioness carries her cub in the Masai Mara National Reserve.

A lioness protects her four-week-old cubs.

GROWING UP LION

Once the cubs are introduced to the pride, they become an active part of the group. Sometimes, they are too active, and male lions will give annoying cubs a gentle swat with a paw. The pride now has three nursing mothers. When they are hungry, cubs search for an empty spot at a female's nipples. Any female with milk will feed a hungry cub, which frees other mothers to go hunting.

By two to three months old, the cubs begin eating meat. Getting a share of the kill can be a challenge. Cubs are usually the last to eat, and older cubs greedily push younger ones aside. However, the youngest cubs are still nursing, so they do not go hungry. Lionesses fully wean their young from drinking milk when they are about eight months old.

Both males and females guard the cubs from attack, but a mother is a fierce protector. At the first sign of danger, she places her body between her cubs and the enemy. She bears her fangs and growls. It takes a serious enemy to continue an attack in the face of a snarling lioness.

For cubs, the time between weaning and adulthood is filled with lessons. Hunting is essential for survival, and cubs must learn the best times and places for hunting. They are taught to set up an

Did You Know?
The lions that live around Lake Manyara in Tanzania are known for their tree climbing. An entire pride will climb into the branches of an acacia or a sausage tree and snooze there all afternoon. The trees provide an escape from herds of elephants and buffalo, as well as from the biting flies that swarm around dung piles.

ambush at a water hole. They also find out how to work together to bring down a zebra. And perhaps most important, they learn to watch out for African buffalo horns, elephant tusks, and hyenas at all times. Both male and female cubs need to learn hunting skills. The males will hunt for themselves during their two-year roaming period. A female must play an active part in the pride's hunting program. Her life and the life of the pride depend on it.

Lions need to drink water to survive.

Chapter Four

In the Family of Lions

About twenty thousand years ago, lions roamed from France and Portugal, across southern Europe, and eastward to India and in parts of the Americas. Lions hunted in the Atlas Mountains of northern Africa and in grasslands far to the south. Today, lions are only found below the Sahara in Africa and in India's Gir Forest National Park. The lands that the lions call home are now limited to less than one-fourth the area they ruled only two thousand years ago. Room for big cats is dwindling.

Big cats are part of the **genus** *Panthera*. This genus, a general class or group of animals, includes lions, leopards, jaguars, and tigers. All lions—African or Asiatic—are the species *Panthera leo.* Today's lions trace their family line back to one shared ancestor that lived two to three million years ago.

AFRICAN LIONS

On a rock ledge in the Kalahari Desert, Namibia, a male lion yawns. Beside him lies a powerful lioness and one of her

Did You Know?
Male lions are the only cats that have manes—and even some lions do not have them. Males begin to grow a thick, obvious mane at about three years old.

cubs. They make a perfect family picture—just what people expect lions to look like.

Once lions roamed across all of Africa, but today, they live only below the Sahara Desert. African lions adapt to a variety of habitats—grassy savannas, open woodlands, marshes, the fringes of deserts, and even the mountains to up to 5,000 meters (16,404 feet). But they do not live in the rain forest. To survive, they need food, water, and a place to sleep.

A mature male lion measures between 2 and 2.5 meters (6 and 8 feet) long, plus tail. Tails range from 0.7 to 1.1 meters (2.3 to 3.5 feet) long and end with a black tuft of hair. Male colors range from tawny to dark browns, and manes may be any color from light brown to black.

At 1.4 to 1.7 meters (4.6 to 5.7 feet) long including the tail, the females are shorter. While males stand about 1.2 meters (4 feet) at the shoulder, females tend to be slightly shorter, about 1 meter (3.3 feet). Females are generally tawny brown in color, with no mane and a sleek, muscular body.

On the savanna, lions prefer wildebeest to any other prey. However, hungry lions will eat just about anything, even **carrion.** All grazing animals—all species

Would You Believe?
When it is available, lions drink water every day. During droughts, lions can go four or five days without drinking. They get fluid from the blood and guts of their prey. Lions in the Kalahari Desert have been seen eating tsama melons to get water.

of antelope, impala, topi, hartebeest, eland, oryx, and zebra—make excellent prey. Lions also hunt for African buffalo, giraffes, or elephants but do so with great care. African buffalo have severely gored many lions during a hunt. Giraffes may look mild, but their sharp, dinner-plate-sized hooves can crush a lion's skull. As for elephants—only very young or very weak elephants make good prey. Individual lions hunting alone will gladly eat reptiles and birds if they can catch them.

Regardless of size, lions are just large cats. Like the family pet, they have thirty teeth—although lion teeth are larger. They have a rough tongue that is ideal for grooming.

A lioness prepares to pounce on a zebra.

Their bone structure is identical to that of Puff or Fluffy, and they are meat eaters. One big difference, however, is in how they sound. A house cat will purr or meow, but a lion can let out a loud roar.

ASIATIC LIONS

According to legend, the **nawab,** or governor, of Junagadh so admired the lions living in the forest around his hunting lodge that he gave them his protection. No one could kill a lion on the nawab's land. In the early 1900s, only thirteen lions existed in this small haven in Gujarat, India. It is from these remaining lions that India's current population of Asiatic lions (*Panthera leo persica*) descended.

The nawab made one of the first efforts to protect Asiatic lions from **extinction.** Today, the nawab's former hunting lodge lies in the center of the Gir Forest National Park, a 1,412-square kilometer (558-square-mile) preserve. The Asiatic lion population has reached nearly five hundred, which is greater than the forest can support.

Male Asiatic lions are smaller and scruffier looking than their African cousins. Adult males typically weigh between

Did You Know?
Occasionally, white lions are born in Timbavati, South Africa. White lions are at a serious disadvantage when hunting. Their coloring makes them stand out against their environment, putting prey on the alert.

150 and 200 kilograms (330 and 440 pounds). Males have shorter manes and a long fold of skin on their bellies.

Adult females weigh between 70 and 135 kilograms (150 and 300 pounds), which is about the same as African lionesses. Females look much like lionesses on the African savanna.

Male Asiatic lions (left) are usually larger than the females (right).

The pride size of Asiatic lions tends to be smaller than that of African prides. Asiatic prides consist of lionesses and cubs. Adult males live alone or in a coalition with another male. Pride size may be limited because prey in the Gir Forest is smaller than prey in Africa. Asiatic lions feed mostly on chital deer, chinkara (a type of gazelle), nilgai (a type of antelope), and wild boar. One chital deer weighs about 55 kilograms (110 pounds), compared to a 440-kilogram (880-pound) zebra. A large pride would need to always be on the hunt.

Today's Asiatic lions face a serious reproductive problem. When the lions came under protection, there were very few left for breeding. After a century with such a small breeding group, Asiatic lions are genetically so close, they could all belong to the same litter. The lions are inbred, which means that they pass on too many **recessive,** or weak, genes. This makes the current population open to disease and physical defects.

Despite these difficulties, the Asiatic lion population continues to grow—which presents a different problem. Humans want to confine the Asiatic lions to the Gir Forest. However, the lions disagree. They do not recognize park borders. They only know that beyond the forest lie cattle—a fast-food pit stop for hungry lions.

Unlike their African counterparts, male Asiatic lions do not belong to the pride.

Chapter Five

The Past, Present, and Future

Scientists have found fossils and ancient bones of cave lions in Greece, France, and Poland. These early lions were relatives of today's lions and lived from 300,000 to 10,000 years ago. They hunted on the **moors** of England and the **steppes** of Russia.

While lions hunted prey, humans hunted lions. In the days of early humans, lions represented a threat to survival, and humans met that threat with spears. In some cultures, killing a lion showed strength and skill. A successful lion hunt marked the transition from boyhood to manhood. These hunts had very little effect on lion populations.

At some point, lion killing became a sport. In Roman days, tens of thousands of lions were released into arenas to be slaughtered by gladiators. More recently, the invention

of rifles threatened lion survival forever. With rifles, humans could kill lions with little danger to themselves. Lion pelts became rugs in people's dens while lion head trophies were hung on the walls.

The slaughter of countless lions continues today. Scientists estimated that in 1996, Africa had from 30,000 to 100,000

This ancient image of lion hunting was created around 98 AD by the Romans.

lions. That number is down to about 23,000—a population decline of 45 to 70 percent in only ten years. Death by disease accounts for some of the population loss. Death by humans and loss of habitat accounts for most of it.

THE PRESENT

Is there room for lions in today's modern world? Natural lion habitat is fast becoming farmland, and conflicts between humans and wild cats ends up with cats on the losing end. Consider the situation from a lion's point of view. Habitat loss equals a loss of prey. When that habitat then becomes a grazing area for cattle, sheep, or goats, big cats kill farm livestock to eat. Wanting to protect their livestock, humans shoot or poison the big cats.

Poaching continues to be a problem, with more than 1,000 lion heads or skins sold on the black market each year. Despite efforts to protect lions, poachers can earn a great deal of money by selling lion body parts. One Ethiopian lion skin sells for about $1,000, or about nine years' wages for an Ethiopian worker. While park rangers try to prevent poaching, there are too few rangers, too much land to protect, and some very clever poachers on the hunt.

Did You Know?
Only three regions of Africa have an estimated lion population of two thousand or more: the Serengeti-Mara in Kenya and Tanzania, the Okavango-Chobe-Hwange in Namibia, and the Kruger National Park and its neighbors in South Africa and Mozambique.

Lions also face serious threats of disease. Like Asiatic lions, African lions living on preserves have a limited genetic pool for breeding. A small gene pool breeds physical weakness in animals. Weaker lions catch diseases, such as tuberculosis and canine **distemper,** which can wipe out an entire regional population. For example, humans and their dogs accidentally introduced canine distemper to Serengeti National Park in 1994. Within a year, nearly one-third of the region's 3,000 lions died from the disease.

THE FUTURE

One hundred years from now, lions may only be found in zoos, national parks, and game preserves. They are losing their natural habitat too quickly.

For Asiatic lions, plans are under way to establish a second lion population in Kuno Wildlife Sanctuary, in Madhya Pradesh. Kuno has been a game preserve since 1981 and can easily support a lion population. It has a variety of habitats that lions enjoy and plenty of prey. Not everyone is keen on having lions as neighbors, however, so an education program has prepared local villages to deal with living with lions next door. To add new genes to the breeding pool, it may be necessary to introduce a handful of African lions into the population.

A veterinarian checks a lion's mouth for signs of disease.

Africa has many game preserves and national parks in which lions live free. However, there is always room for improvement. The African Wildlife Foundation has developed the Lion P.R.I.D.E. Initiative to study and support lion conservation. The programs study lion populations and movements, and the conflicts between humans and lions in three areas of Africa. The goal is to identify and address problems between humans and lions before they happen.

Although there are few bumper stickers shouting "Save the Lion," now is the time to act. Many animal species have come close to extinction because of humans. All too often, these species now exist only in zoos. If human actions can destroy, they can also save. Preserving lions in the wild is essential for maintaining the balance of nature on Africa's savannas and in India's woodlands. The king of beasts deserves the chance to survive.

Glossary

carnivore (CAR-nih-vor) an animal that eats mostly meat

carrion (KAYR-ee-un) dead and rotting flesh

coalition (koh-uh-LIH-shun) a partnership formed for mutual benefit

distemper (dis-TEM-pur) a virus that sickens dogs and cats

escarpment (es-KARP-munt) a cliff

estrus (ESS-truss) a period during which female mammals are ready to mate

extinction (eks-TINK-shun) the state of a plant or animal no longer existing

genes (JEENZ) the chemical substances that determine animal or plant characteristics

genus (JEE-nuhs) a group or class of related animals

instinctively (in-STINK-tiv-lee) acting according to one's natural sense of what is happening with one's body

life span (LIFE SPAN) the total time during which an animal lives

moors (MOORZ) tracts of open land often overgrown with heath or gorse shrubs

nawab (nuh-WAHB) a governor or person of great wealth and power in India

nomadic (noh-MAD-ik) moving regularly; without a fixed home

poaching (POH-ching) to hunt illegally

predator (PREH-duh-tur) an animal that hunts and kills animals for food

prey (PRAY) an animal hunted for food

pride (PRIDE) a group of lions that live and hunt together

recessive (reh-SES-siv) having to do with a nondominant trait

savanna (suh-VAN-nuh) a grassy plain

steppes (STEPZ) vast grasslands in southern and eastern Russia

urine (YUR-in) liquid animal waste

For More Information

Watch It

Explore the Wildlife Kingdom Series: Lions—Kings of Africa, DVD (Monument, CO: LLC Reel Productions, 2005)

Nature: Big Cats, DVD (Chicago: Questar, 2005)

Predators at War, DVD (Washington, DC: National Geographic Video, 2005)

Read It

Anderson, Jill. *Lions*. Minnetonka, MN: NorthWord Press, 2006.

Patent, Dorothy Hinshaw. *Big Cats*. New York: Walker Books for Young Readers, 2005.

Scott, Jonathan and Angela. *Big Cat Diary: Lion*. London: HarperCollins, 2006.

Spilsbury, Richard and Louise. *A Pride of Lions*. Chicago: Heinemann, 2003.

Thomas, Isabel. *Animals Head to Head: Lion vs. Tiger*. Chicago: Raintree, 2006.

Look It Up

Visit our Web page for lots of links about lions:
http://www.childsworld.com/links

Note to Parents, Teachers, and Librarians: We routinely verify our Web links to make sure they are safe, active sites—so encourage your readers to check them out!

The Animal Kingdom
Where Do Lions Fit In?

Kingdom: Animalia

Phylum: Chordata (animals with backbones)

Class: Mammalia

Order: Carnivora

Family: Felidae

Genus: *Panthera*

Species: *Panthera leo*

Index

About the Author

Sophie Lockwood is a former teacher and a longtime writer. She writes textbooks, newspaper articles, and magazine articles. Sophie enjoys writing about animals and their habits. The most interesting part of her research, Sophie says, is learning how scientists apply their knowledge to save endangered species. She lives with her husband in the foothills of the Blue Ridge Mountains.